For Yvonne.

with love

Julia Wroughton.
Bruce Killeen.

Digressions

Digressions

Drawings and Poems
by
Julia Wroughton & Bruce Killeen

STRATHMORE PUBLISHING
LONDON
2008

First published in Great Britain by Strathmore Publishing,
41 Kingsway Place, Sans Walk, London EC1R 0LU, 2008

ISBN 978-0-9550887-5-9

Previously published by the same authors
Evocations
Wood Engravings and Poems
2007

Design and origination by David McLean, London
Typeset in Sabon
Printed in England by Portland Print, Kettering, Northants, NN16 8UN

Published with the assistance of An Tobar Arts Centre,
Argyll Terrace, Tobermory, Isle of Mull, PA75 6PB
Telephone: 01688 302211.   Email: arts@antobar.co.uk
from whom further copies may be obtained.

Foreword

The first book, *Evocations* was about the locality. This one is mostly about distant places. Both represent an attempt to slow down, to stand and stare.

The poems were inspired by the drawings. They are not meant to illustrate; that would be superfluous. They represent one person's response; other people might feel quite differently about them.

Some poems keep quite close to the drawings, others fly off on their own, reach a far country, speak their own language. They are designed to be read aloud.

There are two kinds of drawing. A sketch-like note to catch a sensation, or a more-considered statement based upon reflection as well as observation. Nearly all were made on the spot.

B. K.

Contents

A Winter Tree

Concordia discors ... Horace

She welcomes like a hostess
a variety of guests;
how can these disparate characters
ever coalesce?

Ancient barn and recent car
and washing on the line quite still,
contradictory forms made by man,
by God and God knows who
should shatter any composition
but here they don't, they don't...
discords marvellous in harmony.

Hebridean
Audrey at the Window

The way she stands tells all
I clasp her from behind
she does not move
she's out there on the islands
that twenty years ago she fled
I need uncertainty she said,
dissolute or elegant
broken promises or not.

But not now I say,
she does not hear,
let me arrange the tesserae
make my own mosaic
so keep your distance Patrick boy,
our childhood game was over long ago.

She's out there on the islands
balancing regret
the gleaming sand
the city windows
the dancing-floor –
look what we've missed I say,
are missing still;
she does not hear,
the way she stands tells all.

Giardini

Light comes off the sea
touches momentarily
archway, statue, tree –
the detail in the structure
restraint in sensuosity.

Gabriel Fauré in the garden,
a dollar-princess in tow
(the generous Wineretta)
she gave more than money though
to make that music
the deepest sharing of their lives.

Do patrons have to patronize?
there is a giving of the means
there is a giving of the love.

This is a busy city
a showy sort of place
rope-factories football-stadiums
car-ferries demo-men.

By the archway, statue, tree,
I think of Fauré's music always
(a breeze comes off the sea,
long grasses lift
a flag flies almost straight)
the detail in the structure,
restraint in sensuosity.

Scattered Walls

They scribble across Cumbrian hills
in accordance with the pitch and toss,
lost at first in layered mist
found again in sudden light
obdurate definers of green spaces
they tolerate no soft option –
there is no arguing with a wall.

The stones are found
as words are for a sonnet
by instinct and by stealth:
sometimes they fall apart
advance too far, too straight,
wriggle in a wrong direction
find firm ground too late

and then at last cohesion;
every stone has found its place –
the cadence of completion.

Hatted Lady

Make time stand still
or stand it on its head
forget those past mistakes
or future dread
the face-saving
and the guilt,
the call of men
the coo of women
the ways of desperation.

Find only a corner
of the house
where you can be
for ever, still.

Here, only the artist's grammar speaks;
the curves are curves to draw
echoes of construction
the small curve
across the hat
along the bowl
down the throne-like chair:
leave the hatted lady
exactly where she is.

Conversazione

...and Gianne went to Mestre,
and as you know, we had to close
but did you hear about Alfredo
at the hospitale?
He met a girl who hurt her wrist – and what do you
suppose?
He touched her, dear
(he told me this himself)
one touch and he was gone.
They're in Paris now I do believe
I'll tell you if I hear
and...

Westerly

The wind, all fingers and thumbs
has flicked the benches over quite
denounced there usefulness till kingdoms come.

But why not re-instate,
watch those southern islands yet again,
sea through a wine-glass darkly?

Planner's Bench

Presences?
two at least
if the tray's report
be accurate.

Channels of corrugation
extend blue shadow-lines
across the casual porch
late light touches corners
the sturdy bench,
the small teapot
where two cups
might have stood.

The planner's bench
is not for dreaming,
nostalgia's almost
held at bay.

The anxious planners
stride off-course,
find at last
the cliff-top view
half watch
the descending sun;
they talk of Wall Street
and the Bourse.

In The Park

The child is in a hurry to be away
has several times attempted onward motion.
Three is never a good number
always one so sad, reflecting, not noticing
has never seen the sunniness of the place
only felt its grandiose solemnity.

Mother is young, fully in command
did she leave the oven on?
better to go back, come out again?

This the centre of a great city
Berlioz lived here, Matisse,
Chagall for a time.

In the park every bench is occupied
people have forgotten things
but they've flung away ambition
are happy to be unhappy
not quite sure of the difference.

The statue yearns to reach the sky
the little boy, the Mother,
have no such futile urge:
feet are on the ground round here
a place for the incurably sane.

To Break a Fall

The road is clear enough
and lost again,
mist rising, falling,
contours re-drawn,
voices out at sea:
the estuary sends back the clouds,
rubs them out, returns them softened and more spread.

Malcolm has gone ahead
reached the church
is climbing high
an insect that might
break
in two
plunge to death
sand not soft enough
to break a fall
'Look Auntie, human bones!'

The Greater Thrust
recalling Norman Douglas

There is always the awkward one
who stands out from the crowd
would like to join but cannot;
tries of course, not hard enough.

Throw a dozen teaspoons
across a kitchen-table
the chance of light
will make a prince of one
a dunce of many:
democracy is man-made
an indoor plant,
chance, without the window.

In the forest
an equality of trees
torments and teases
more than mildly threatening,
be like us or else...
torments and teases.

The lighter bark
contains the stronger sap
the innocent, the greater thrust:
keep your edges intact
said Uncle Norman,
his was not the path of righteousness
nor self-deception
his little game:
he washed his brains
on the Island of Capri,
no mirror to distort.

The Prize

The sea now
rarely comes this far
but sometimes
like the playful cat
it really is lingers
to inspect the prize
but half-preserved,
the twisted rib-cage
the casual dislocation
the death-throws that repeat
the waves unfolding will
as does the gentle branch enclosing
acknowledge by its framing
such displays of ferocity and skill.

The Pantheist

Nolde I suggest,
of profiles the most Nordic
knew how to die,
surrender that is
to sea and sky
'the clouds are my friends' –
the final gesture of a pantheist.

Mondrian couldn't,
wouldn't do it,
imposed his right-angle,
his chilly prison-bar.

'I am only interested
in the works of man,'
(he might have said)
Isaiah Berlin pre-echo;
nothing ever grows
if we pull out all the roots,
if we look the other way.

The sea that lunges at the rock
brings up its heavies to demolish,
hasn't far to go to reach that house
pour its wall with glistening foam
strike flat its trivial cube
the curve is mightier than the line:
Nolde's life is worth the losing.

Beyond Appearance

Those who dream are labourers and co-creators
of all that is happening in the universe Heraclitus

We can only write what's right for us to write
it would be wrong
to end our song

be it short or long
with honey or with treacle
if we'd seen the Russian tanks
or compromised with people.

Hypocritical to turn political
if our life is calm as cardboard
tranquil as the sea
seeing it has many moods,
a complex personality.

Neruda went political
to improve the human lot
Holub fought the lyrical
the magic and the charm
but both were metaphorical
whether they admitted it or not
viewed the world with great alarm
found a sweetness deep within.

Butterflies are out of touch
they barely last a month
to terminate their flight,
to cast a tiny shadow,
leave a residue of light.

Montalcino

Incoherent, doesn't unify at all
architects hate this square I'm told
uncomfortable assemblage, one friend said:
so perhaps conversation there is fraught
strange the arcade is high enough
there's space for you to breath,
no beating down of mankind here.

So why are orders sotto voce
commands at whisper-level?
She stands to attention to obey
is there mockery in that pose?
She will not enjoy her walk to-day.

Not straight down to Cesare's, you promise?
and we don't need cheeses anyway,
the vegetables I leave to you
but they won't have what we want,
I'll bring the wine, but I'll be late.

No beating down of mankind here:
the watcher in the boots shrugs shoulders
doesn't know the language,
walks away.

Hard Edge

They jerk across though,
free from hieroglyphics
yellow sheep on a ground
of yellow chippings
clockwork to re-wind,
carvings re-engrave,
just below the house
(tired eyes hurt
by this aridity).

The sea, the sky,
play no part,
no softening of the edges.

Buttressed, tumble-tiled
shelter still is offered,
man-made element returning
more than given:
sheep and building know endurance,
forced upon them shared nobility,
survival by their own volition.

Sainte-Mère
Trees and Towers

The part
as delicate
as the whole,
the tracery
of leaf,
of tree,
December frost
silver ghosts
question marks
poised uncertainly.
Substantial
all the way
not a pause
in upward thrust
not a wobble
not a break,
ninety feet
the tallest tower
in Gascony
they say:
and through
the mist
the crosses cut,
the cross of Christ,
the bowman's cross,
for war, for peace,
for contemplation:

a place
to stand and stare,
to celebrate
in disbelief
the pencilled line of Pyrenees.

Le Bouscarel

O yes, it's breaking-up all right
it'll last a thousand years –
drive a nail into the timber if you can.

The massive beams are almost pretty now,
theatrical, degenerate, in dis-array,
soft violet in the evening light,
walls of apricot, shutters broken green,
long grass pale honey-gold.

Try the gallery (its safe enough);
a line of ancient stamps, of penny blacks –
is there someone up there anyway,
a figure near the upper door?
no, this is not a haunted place;
no menace here, no tale to tell
except the view through little squares,
the endless oceanic waves of Lot.

Master craftsmen worked here once
with love, with strength and with finesse;
structure as decoration – the final synthesis.

O it's breaking up all right
it'll last a thousand years
the toughness of cathedrals,
they could have built Rouen.

The Precipice

The wind will elbow through its way,
the rain erode as is its wont
with more patient equanimity.

The sculptured cliffs far overhead
stage-boxes stacked below
scraggy trees bear witness
or did bear witness long ago
to desperate scenes enacted here.

Where the valley-end becomes a precipice
the Moorish invaders made their final stand
Spanish Catholic armies drove them off:
some say a ghostly dissonance
can still be heard but I hear nothing,
nothing, except below the cliff
and all the ravaged way along,
constant echoes of the blackbird's song.

The Black Madonna

In the heat of early evening
the church bell chimes seven twice
the mountains hold the echoes in
for a long time they reverberate,
diminish slowly with the dying light.

Once near here,
working by the olive trees,
a ploughman found a black Madonna
a figure of great beauty it was claimed.

She has a place now forever holy
in the nearby monastery of Lluc
displayed in all her silver finery.

Pilgrims flock and money flows.
Does she ever think, I wonder
of cursing that poor ploughman?

Washing Day
April 19th 2005

Parts of Naples win first prize
the Giudecca runs it pretty close
enough clean sail they hoist
to drag the streets far out
leave rolling-stock behind

but here the little lady –
not so little after all,
makes compositions all her own
for every day is different
in this corner by the church.

An albatross, annunciation,
the dance from La Calinda,
a wedding group,
procession on a bridge,
a row of blue more densely packed
more menacing by far;
the order's never kept the same
and when she feels she's finished,
surveyed it all from sideways
as a decent critic should, –
what then? What then?

Every city bell is ringing –
she has her own wide screen of course –
white arms are stretched in blessing
'I Papa!' then she cries, 'I Papa!'

The new Papa has been chosen.

Jacob's Angels

I thought it was a refuge,
a breakaway, a levitation,
from the cheerful pandemonium down below.

What a little miracle
to find these steps to heaven
(where else can they lead?)
out of chaos into order
through the menace of the trees
above the pandemonium down below.

They call it
The Cesspool of Europe,
renowned for acts of violence,
but the men who built these steps
were calm enough;
with what precision every line is cut,
what care, what exactitude,
hands which can be subtle could be kind;
brutality and gentleness
can they co-exist
in the pandemonium down below?

Elegance of step,
nobility of urn
the plants so deftly tended,
halting-points of no return;
the way ahead is always upwards, up
from the pandemonium down below.

In this coming darkness
where still the heat prevails,
slender shadows criss-cross
stripe the paving edge,
the wings of Jacob's angels,
descending, ascending
above the pandemonium down below.

Interior
Rajasthan

Sudden coolness of the hall
    (great blades rotate)
shadows march and counter-march
shafts of light between
white figure briefly caught
    (detail of the collar)
other figures slender, dark
motionless along the wall.

Water from a distant tap
    the cry of birds
    the creak of palm
    a dog far off
grandfather clocks strike all together
    (someone's great collection)
 sounds diminish, overlap.

The more you listen
the deeper goes the silence
the more you tell the time
the more time dies

    (the white ghost is exorcised)

Can sounds be with silence shared –
    a voice destroy?

Pushkar Fair

At Pushkar Fair
they make the camels-up
(its true my friend, they really do)
scarves, sari, tunics, rickshaws
motorised or not
all the local colour,
the camel drains the lot;
lifts up a foot
looks down its nose
wins the prize;
retains somehow
the noble pose,
crosses desert looking good.

What more to life than that?
a proper guided ride of course
no idiot on his own,
picked up so carefully
put down with such respect.

At Pushkar Fair
they keep up this pretence
so come my friend,
let's cross the desert looking good.

Not Too Far

A Man Could Stand Up
(Whose title that –
was it Fordy?)

Under these branches
there's room
to dodge unbending
(but only just)
easy for you
my careless Lilliputian
you'll know the wood
from the trees.

Bend low, bend low
we'll make a run for it:
confinement and release
on equal terms
neck and neck,
breakneck for the asking
so choose the obvious
and make a run for it
my daring Lilliputian

through light and shade
umbrageous, crepuscular,
select an exit-point
the ways ahead are infinite,
infinite the tunnellings:

everything is possible
but not too far
too far in this enchanted place
a man could not stand up:
you might survive,
survive alone,
my darling Lilliputian.

The Herd – Pastorale

The livestock market describes them well
by hundreds at a time
in heavy black-and-white typography –
their future is well-planned.

They move in groups like tourists
noticed and unseen
black-and-white beneath black trees
lost and found continuous, ambiguous;
no sunny terminus for them
unlike the bather through the shallow sea,
the patient basking on the balcony,
the climber ever looking upwards
a bar of gold across his neck:
no angel comes to warm their back.

They cannot ever know
the pleasure they have given
the life-force they have spent
a moment's grace unconsciously transmitted
unstoppable, indifferent.

The Gardener

I love great houses
with long libraries
and gardens full of statues;
I love as much old bombsites
or a waste lot;
anywhere not goggled-at;
a flower that struggles
against the odds,
a scrap of poster tugging to be off
(a bird, a tiger, Andromeda)
the life that's gone
the life to come.

For you, the gardener said –
she took the quill
began to draw,
upon compulsion really,
the towers, parterres,
the sleepy lions off- guard;
symbols, images that impress
open mouths and eyes,
pockets with equal readiness.

Lovely to draw and lovely too
Robert's abandoned corner
he hasn't time to tend
tall grasses sway in unison
trees float or spread for light.

Robert haunts this part
enjoys the absence
of adornment or display –
his compost-heaps they say
are the best in southern France.

The Château

The grand entrance pillars,
the grand clouds tethered:
a last light sharpens
the end of the long drive
like a clasp-knife –
it will go out shortly,
close with a severing snap.

Ancient, innocent, vulnerable,
the front porch crouches
like a frightened rabbit
with a dunce's cap:
towers on every corner stand
like guardsmen with an off-duty look
a massive keep, six levels defendable
wears a delicate bonnet for a silent bell.

Trees massing forces on the right
rows of windows perched like birds:
will it all go out shortly
with a severing snap?

Only a solitary horse
treads warily the upper slope.

From whose fair picture-book
was this page torn?

Early Arrival

I look at other people's poems
(what foolishness forsooth)
and find they are so sad
they write about the things that count
they go deeper, deeper far
than what I write or seem to write.

Seems madam, I know not seems,
but seems is all it is, it is:
I think I've come to grips with life
but I always miss it like a bus
I chase illusions, possibilities,
I conjecture with delights
but it is sadness I must find
the real Life that somewhere is.

Sadness should not be difficult
there isn't far to go
three friends died this year
all from the same afflicted town
I've shoved it off the map,
what price other people
if my good friends have gone?
It is, it is no longer seems,
I can only cope with this,
this much real reality.

The front gate has just blown open
the driveway is a lake
and there poor Giles
who has just arrived
sees his latest hat afloat
which makes me smile – I could make a poem about
that:
let us begin at once –
Hurry dear, Giles is at the gate.

The Mountains Laugh

Again the mountains laugh
fight the gale and laugh
the waterfalls are flashing teeth
rocks send signals down the line
but higher up the river turns
blows upwards into sky,
soft as gauze, a muslin dress,
lifting, falling with
every tactic of the wind.

When suddenly the storm abates,
forms replenished in the crystal air,
the chimney stack asserts authority
re-instates the status quo.

The chastened fall but meekly steps its way
lifts up its dress for every stone
heavier, more opaque than muslin was:
calmness now is universal
sobriety the only rule,
elements in collusion.

Aegean
Mary at the Window

I am one of those dim creatures
I suppose said Mary once,
who need to think before they speak
or search before they find
but in the searching
(slow but never desperate, sir)
you have no idea what depth
of Trojan treasure I discover.

I think you are wonderful Mary dear, he said
I love the absent dreamy look,
I guess your patient inner strength,
but how about spontaneity for God's sake,
giving way for once, joining in?

I am not sure where I want to go,
or where I've been so far
Art School was fog and ice for me
I couldn't see my way
I need light and clarity and space
Samos and Skopelos and Ithaka
I shall go there some day surely
even if my little Grecian bag
has lost its Trojan treasure...

No, I go alone. Mother used to say,
Wake up Mary, you silly girl
you'll die of dreaming and so I may, I may –
perhaps I have already.

The Promise

He is perpetually round the corner, sir
Martin Chuzzlewit

Thanks be to God
for corners left to turn
for turnings left in place
> from
> driver
> postman
> ploughman
> businessman
> invalid
and particularly from Chevy Slyme.

To all those that make the corner
but never of their own sweet will

the promise of a sunlit garden,
a mountain to protect
the northern flank,
a wall of silence
in perpetuity
but where is perpetuity?

In northern Scotland
dare I say,
braving the Atlantic
or the chilly Pentland Firth.

We'll leave untouched
the secrets of this corner
shake hands with Chevy Slyme
return the way we never came
contrive our final rhyme.

Julia Wroughton studied at Colchester School of Art and the Royal College of Art in London. She taught in several Art Schools and later founded Inniemore School of Painting on the Isle of Mull where she still lives and paints. She has exhibited frequently in London, Bristol and Edinburgh and has paintings in private and public collections in Britain and abroad.

Bruce Killeen read English at Oxford but after an extended visit to Italy became particularly interested in painting. He has exhibited at the Royal Academy and the Royal West of England Academy and he has had Solo exhibitions with the Artists' International Association and the Drian Galleries in London. He was a tutor at the Royal Academy Schools and an Art Correspondent for the *Guardian*. He now works on the Isle of Mull.